How To Listen To Money

Katie Canty

ISBN: 9798376049426

Copyright 2023

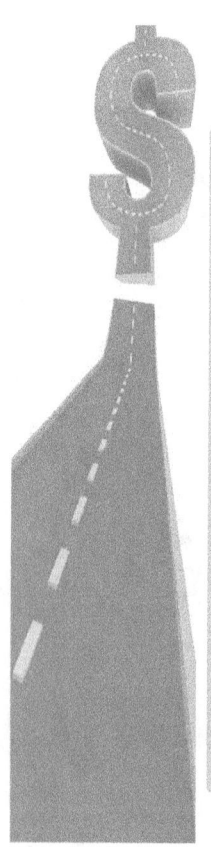

TABLE OF CONTENTS

Relationship Investments....page 5

How To Be Rich....page 24

How To Prosper....page 41

What To Do With Wealth....page 52

Beyond Money Investments...page 68

Introduction

Everyone with a credit debit card, this book is for you. It is for the invisible poor, the poor, and the rich.

**A new billionaire says God is good. Want to know more about how good and great God still is?

**Relax and enjoy more of the rich life right now. This book can be your friendly, rich companion and is usually readable in 25-35 minutes.

**Get and keep a positively rich life—even during rough and tough times.

With each affirmation and quote that you read, may there be a rich blessing there for you.

How To Profit Relationship Investments

A woman has the greatest and richest gifts from God that no man can have.

A man has the greatest, riches gifts from God that no woman can have.

Wealth creation: It is God's amazing gift to women and to men.

There is a difference. Choose intelligently. The woman who wants you to be her rich husband, or the woman who wants to be your rich wife.

Choose wisely. There is a difference. The man who wants you to be his rich wife, or the man who wants to be your rich husband.

Make sure that your vision and mission to get and use money has God's approval in the plan.

If the rich life, causes ungodly behavior that causes wonderful family and friends, including the family dog, not to want to be in a person's presence, unless paid to do so--then what good are riches.

Charity begins at home.

Money does not buy true, genuine, real love. This is always true. Don't let your money try to buy it.

Friending God back, yields a relationship with the best kinds of returns that last far beyond a lifetime.

Three things will last forever: faith, hope, and love--and the greatest of these is love.

1Corinthians 13:13

> For where two or three are gathered together in my name, there am I in the midst of them.
>
> Matthew 18:20

Blessed is the man who walks not in the counsel of the ungodly, nor stands in the path of sinners, nor sits in the seat of the scornful.

Psalms 1:1

Make no friendship with an angry man. And with a furious man thou shalt not go: Lest thou learn his ways and get a snare to thy soul.

Proverbs 22:24-25

He that walketh with wise men shall be wise...

Proverbs 13:20

Draw nigh to God, and he will draw nigh to you.

James 4:8

How To Be Rich

God's divine providence or a winning mega lottery ticket: No purchase necessary for one of these.

Hard work and riches can be seen shaking hands very, very often.

Memory overload and screen time over stimulation can silently deplete riches little by little, swipe by swipe. Take back control of device controls.

The surest way to get rich and richer, but not necessarily the quickest or the easiest way, is to sincerely love God; put God first.

It is the blessing of the Lord that makes rich, and he adds no sorrow to it.

Proverbs 10:22

But seek first the kingdom of God and his righteousness, and all these things will be added to you.

Matthew 6:33

Godly citizens cause a city to prosper.

Proverbs 11:11

> There is treasure in being good, but trouble dogs the wicked.
>
> Proverbs 15:10

Better is a little with the fear of the Lord than great treasure and trouble with it.

Proverbs 15:16

The wiseman saves for the future, but the foolish man spends whatever he gets.

Proverbs 21:29

> For what shall it profit a man, if he shall gain the whole world, and lose his own soul?
>
> Mark 8:36

The kingdom of heaven is like a treasure hidden in the field, which a man found and hid again, and from joy over it he goes and sells all that he has and buys that field.

Matthew 13-44

For where your treasure is, there your heart will be also.

Luke 12:24

The reward of humility and the fear of the Lord are riches, honor, and life.

Proverbs 22-4

My son, keep my words store up my commandments within you.

Proverbs 7:1

The rich rules over the poor, and the borrower is the slave of the lender.

Proverbs 22:7

I can do all things through Jesus Christ--him who gives me strength.

Philippians 4:13

How To Prosper

There is a DNA code for prosperity. The "D" stands for divine destiny. Your code is in the Bible.

GPS: God's Plan of Salvation is a treasure map for "finding everything," not "losing anything" that God has for your good." Many blessings follow followers of this type of GPS.

CPR—Christ, Prayer, and Repentance

CPR is how the rich and poor begin to save themselves as needed from falling into a state of spiritual bankruptcy.

God, our Father, gifts his human children with gifts to be rich in every possible way. The catch is for his children to try keep God's commandments in every possible way.

We can be rich with or without a rich Dad by keeping our Father God in our activities of daily living.

The more money and possessions you have, the richer you are. This in not always true.

Therefore, keep the words of this covenant and do them, that you may prosper in all that you do.

Deuteronomy 29:9

Whoever pursues righteousness and love finds life, prosperity and honor.

Proverbs 20:21

Blessed is the one who does not walk in step with the wicked or stand in the way that sinners take or sit in the company of mockers, but whose delight is in the law of the LORD, and who meditates on his law day and night. That person is like a tree planted by streams of water, which yields its fruit in season and whose leaf does not wither. Whatever they do prospers.

Psalms 1:13

This book of the law shall not depart from your mouth, but you shall meditate on it day and night, so that you may be careful to do according to all that is written in it. For then you will make your way prosperous, and then you will have good success.

Joshua 1:8

And observe what the Lord your God requires. Walk in obedience to him, and keep his decrees and commands, his laws and regulations, as written in the Law of Moses. Do this so that you may prosper in all you do and wherever you go.

1Kings 2:3

What To Do With Wealth

Yes, good health is one of the most, if not the most important forms of wealth. The essential thing to do is to take care of your health—protect the mind, heart, and soul. Keep it clean.

Don't get poor. Know when the costs of money costs too much. The Bible tells when.

When it comes to the newest types of computer generated money, know what to expect before you connect.

Approach God with the right spirit, heart and mind when bringing your tithes and offerings.

Blessings, abundance, and provisions: Send God a thank you note by sharing with the poor that God directs you to bless.

> So, whatever you eat or drink, or whatever you do, do everything for the glory of God.
>
> Corinthians 11:31

Be not wise in your own eyes, fear the Lord and turn away from evil. This will mean health for your flesh and vigor for your bones.

Proverbs 37:8

Honor the Lord with your wealth, with the first fruits of all your crops, then your barns will be filled to overflowing, and your vats will brim over with new wine.

Proverbs 39:10

Whoever sows sparingly will also reap sparingly, and whoever sows generously will also reap generously.

1Corinthians

> Whoever is generous to the poor lends to The Lord, and He will repay him for his deed.
>
> Proverbs 19:17

Do not store up for yourselves treasures on earth, where moth and decay destroy, and thieves break in and steal. But store up treasures in heaven, where neither moth nor decay destroys, nor thieves break in and steal.

Matthew 6:19

God gives some people wealth, possessions and honor, so that they lack nothing their hearts desire, but God does not grant them the ability to enjoy them. And strangers enjoy them instead. This is meaningless, a grievous evil.

Ecclesiastes 6:2

But those who desire to be rich fall into temptation, into a snare, into many senseless and harmful desires that plunge people into ruin and destruction. For the love of money is a root of all kinds of evils. It is through this craving that some have wandered away from the faith and pierced themselves with many pangs.

1Timothy 9:10

As for the rich in this present age, charge them not to be haughty, nor to set their hopes on the uncertainty of riches, but on God, who richly provides us with everything to enjoy. They are to do good, to be rich in good works, to be generous and ready to share, thus storing up treasure for themselves as a good foundation for the future, so that they may take hold of that which is truly life.

1Timothy 6:17

A cheerful heart is good medicine, but a crushed spirit dries up the bones.

Proverbs 31:17.

Beyond Money Affirmations for the Greatest Profit

Do not give up on your dreams of the rich life. After all, if you live God's dream for your life, there is no such thing as the impossible dream.

Yes, mastering the art of listening to God is the best thing to do to both build back better and to make great again.

If I wrong God to get anything, then I have truly lost everything.

Yes, if respect is no longer being served, I can and will excuse myself and leave the table—regardless of whether it is a poor or a rich person's table.

The one investment that matters most is to be right with God.

ABOUT THE AUTHOR

Dr. Katie Canty, Ed.D.
is on a collaborative
mission to spread tech & Bible wealth
among multi-generational
populations worldwide
--1 byte at a time.

www.ingramcontent.com/pod-product-compliance
Lightning Source LLC
Chambersburg PA
CBHW050255220526
45465CB00002B/696